World of Wonder
RAIN FOREST
ANIMALS

Published in Great Britain in 2008 by
The Salariya Book Company Ltd
25 Marlborough Place, Brighton BN1 1UB

ISBN-13: 978-0-531-20452-8 (lib. bdg.)   978-0-531-20543-3 (pbk.
ISBN-10: 0-531-20452-9 (lib. bdg.)   0-531-20543-6 (pbk.)

All rights reserved.
Published in 2008 in the United States
by Children's Press
An imprint of Scholastic Inc.

A CIP catalog record for this book is available
from the Library of Congress.

Printed and bound in China.
Printed on paper from sustainable sources.

The **golden potto** lives
in African rain forests.
At night it feeds on
insects by picking them
off twigs and leaves, or by
catching them as they fly past.

Author and artist: Carolyn Franklin is
a graduate of Brighton College of Art,
England, specializing in design and
illustration. She has worked in animation
and advertising, and has written and
illustrated many natural-history books
for children.

Editor: Stephen Haynes

PAPER FROM

SUSTAINABLE FORESTS

World of Wonder
Rain Forest Animals

Written and illustrated by

Carolyn Franklin

Squirrel monkey

children's press
An Imprint of Scholastic Inc.

NEW YORK • TORONTO • LONDON • AUCKLAND • SYDNEY
MEXICO CITY • NEW DELHI • HONG KONG
DANBURY, CONNECTICUT

Contents

Green tree frog

What Is a Rain Forest?

Emergent layer

Canopy

Understory

Forest floor

A rain forest is a forest of trees that grow very close together in a part of the world where it is warm and there is a lot of rain. Many amazing plants and animals live in the rain forests.

A rain forest can be divided into four layers: the **forest floor**, the **understory**, the **canopy**, and the **emergent** layer. Different plants grow on each layer, and these plants support many different animals.

5

Cardinal tetra

Swordtail

Silver dollar

Electric eel

Do Fish Live in Rain Forests?

Yes: more than 1,500 different types of fish live in the **Amazon** River, which flows through the South American rain forests. There are tiny, brightly colored fish called tetra, huge stingrays, and giant catfish.

Neon tetra

Angelfish

The largest hunter in the Amazon River is the black caiman, a kind of alligator. It grabs, drowns, and finally swallows its **prey** whole.

Spotted head-stander

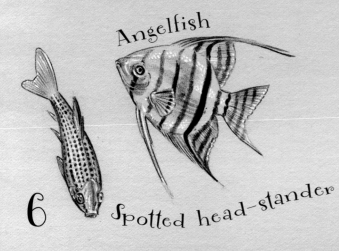

Scary Fish!

Red piranha hunt in large groups,
feeding mainly on other fish. However,
if a big land animal becomes stuck in the
water, a school of piranha will attack it,
eating everything but its bones.

Red-tailed catfish

Red piranha

Stingray

Chocolate cichlid

Mata-mata turtle

Hoatzin

Smelly Birds

Hoatzin are birds that live in thick forests near rivers and lakes. They eat mainly leaves. This bulky diet not only makes it difficult for them to fly, but also makes them smell bad!

Can a Tapir Snorkel?

A tapir has a snout similar to an elephant's trunk, which it uses for reaching and pulling plants into its mouth. When frightened, it can hide under the water and use its snout like a snorkel.

Alligator

Tapir

Paca

Anaconda

Goliath bird-eating spider

The goliath bird-eating spider really does eat small birds! It also feeds on frogs, large insects, lizards, and even small mammals.

How Big Is the Largest Spider?

The dark forest floor, covered in dead and dying leaves, is home to all sorts of ants, termites, millipedes, beetles, worms, and spiders. The largest spider in the world is the goliath bird-eating spider—it can be as big as a dinner plate!

Millipede

True or False?
Leafcutter ants make tents out of the pieces of leaf they cut.

Answers on page 31

How Many Legs?
Most millipedes have between 80 and 400 legs. As they get older they may grow more legs.

Leafcutter ants

11

Why Are the Tree Roots So Big?

The layer of soil in a rain forest is thin, so tree roots cannot grow deep down into the ground. Instead, the trees have big **buttress roots** that grow out from the side of their trunks, and help hold the enormous trees in place.

True or False?
Rain forests contain more than half of the world's huge number of plant and animal **species**.

Answers on page 31

Hummingbird

Postman butterfly

Tamandua

Armadillo

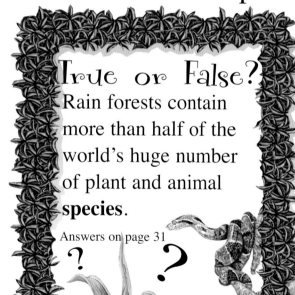

Vine

Creeper

Creepers!
Long, thin creepers, vines, and lianas grow up toward the sunlit canopy, using the large trees for support.

Liana

Coati

Buttress roots

13

Three-toed sloth

Do Sloths Turn Green?

The three-toed sloth uses its strong claws to cling upside down in the branches of the canopy. Tiny plants, too small to see, grow in the sloth's damp fur, making it look slightly green.

Keel-billed toucan

True or False?

A tree porcupine has a special tail that it waves in the air to keep itself cool.

? ?

Answers on page 31

Sounds Like a Frog!

A keel-billed toucan makes a sound just like a frog. Toucans eat mainly fruit, but they also eat lizards, snakes, and even the eggs of smaller birds.

Tree porcupine

Do Snakes Eat Birds?

An emerald tree boa is a large, green snake. Boas don't have teeth for chewing, so they swallow birds and other prey whole!

Jaguar

One Bite!

A jaguar has very strong jaws and kills its prey with one bite. It climbs up into a tree, then pounces on its prey from a hiding place among the branches. Jaguars have powerful muscles, and long claws on their front paws.

Emerald tree boa

Blue tanager

Can Frogs Live in Trees?

Yes! High up in the branches of rain forest trees live tiny poison arrow frogs.

Bromeliad

Special plants called **bromeliads** grow in the canopy. They hold pools of rainwater in their leaves. Poison arrow frogs carry their **tadpoles** to the pools to feed.

Dragonfly

clearwing moth

The rain forest canopy towers as high as 150 feet above the ground. In places where the sun shines through, plants like ferns and mosses grow on the tree branches.

Fern

Moss

Poison arrow frog

Tadpoles

How Big Is a Monkey Family?

Large groups of up to 300 squirrel monkeys may live together. The group spreads through the different levels of the forest to search for food.

True or False?
The harpy eagle eats monkeys, but prefers to catch sloths.

Answers on page 31

squirrel monkey

Macaw

Harpy eagle

Which Monkeys Have Red Faces?

The red uakari is a monkey with a bright
red face and head. These shy animals
live in the forest canopy. They eat seeds
and nuts with their strong jaws.

Red uakari

21

Woolly monkey

What Lives in the Tallest Trees?

The tallest trees, called emergents, grow high above the thick, dark canopy. Up to 200 feet tall, they are home to many types of birds, bats, and monkeys.

Vultures have good senses of smell and sight, and can spot prey in the forest far below. Vultures prefer to eat animals that are already dead, or even rotting!

King vultures

True or False?
20% of the world's bird species live in the trees of the Amazon rain forest.

Answers on page 31

Vine snake

Hummingbird

Fragrant orchid

Bat

Instead of growing colorful leaves or petals, some plants produce strong smells. At night their scent attracts fruit bats and insects such as night-flying moths.

Do Animals Hunt at Night?

Yes! Many animals, such as the owl monkey, certain bats, sloths, and insects, sleep during the day. At dusk they wake up and go in search of food. The owl monkey has enormous eyes that help it see in the dark.

Hawk moth

Owl monkey

Red-eyed
tree frog

25

Do People Live in Rain Forests?

Yes: for thousands of years people have lived in rain forests. The Yanomami Indians still live in parts of the South American rain forest. They use spears, longbows, and poison-tipped arrows to catch fish, monkeys, and wild pigs. They also grow plantains, which are similar to bananas.

The Yanomami live in hundreds of small villages dotted around the Amazon rain forest. Their homes are large, palm-covered huts that they share with other families. The forest provides them with all they need to live.

Quetzal

Orange-winged
Amazon Parrot

True or False?
The Yanomami people put poison made from berries on the tips of their arrows.

? ?

Answers on page 31

27

Will There Always Be Rain Forests?

Each year huge areas of rain forest are destroyed. Areas are cleared of trees so that crops can be grown or roads and cities can be built. Trees are cut down because wood is needed, or because there is a useful mineral under the ground.

Red-eyed tree frog

Many types of frogs live in the rain forests today. But if we continue to destroy the forests, these frogs and many other incredible animals will die.

True or False?

Rain forests can help prevent flooding in some places.

Answers on page 31

Rain forests are very important. Many of their plants can be used as medicines. Rain forests also provide rainfall and help control temperatures. Without rain forests, the world's weather would change.

29

Useful Words

Amazon A huge river in South America. It is not the longest river in the world, but it is the one with the most water.

Bromeliads A family of plants that includes the pineapple.

Buttress roots Roots that grow out sideways from the trunk of a tree to help support it in thin soil.

Canopy The second-highest part of the rain forest. It includes the tops of all but the tallest trees.

Emergent A very tall tree that grows above the forest canopy.

Forest floor The lowest level of the rain forest, where many insects and other creatures live among the decaying leaves.

Fer-de-lance

Prey Animals that are killed and eaten by other animals.

Species The name that scientists use to refer to an individual type of plant or animal.

Tadpole A baby frog.

Understory The second-lowest level of the forest, formed by small trees and shrubs.

The fer-de-lance is the most dangerous snake found in the South American rain forest.

A chameleon from Africa shoots out a long tongue to trap its prey.

Chameleon

Answers

Page 11   FALSE! The leafcutter ants chew off pieces of leaf and carry them to their underground nests. There they build "compost heaps" that grow fungus. They feed this fungus to their young.

Page 12   TRUE! Rain forests cover only a very tiny part (6% or less) of the Earth's surface, yet more than half of the world's different types of plants and animals can be found in these incredible forests.

Page 15   FALSE! The tree porcupine uses its special tail when climbing trees. If attacked, the porcupine may bite back or sit down and shake its sharp quills at its enemy. Or it might stamp its feet and then roll up into a ball for protection.

Page 20   TRUE! Harpy eagles fly over the canopy snatching monkeys, lizards, and sloths from the treetops.

Page 23   TRUE! As many as 20% (one in five) of the world's bird species live in the tall rain forest trees that surround the Amazon River.

Page 27   FALSE! They use the deadly skin of poison arrow frogs. Forest people put the poison on their arrow tips when they go hunting.

Page 29   TRUE! Plants take carbon dioxide gas from the air. Too much of this gas makes the earth and the air around it hotter. Without rain forest plants, the earth would get warmer and the ice at the North and South poles would melt. Low-lying land would then flood.

Index

(Illustrations are shown in **bold type**.)